An Awakening of Love

A PEEK BEYOND THE VEIL

SILVIA PERCHUK

authorHOUSE®

AuthorHouse™
1663 Liberty Drive
Bloomington, IN 47403
www.authorhouse.com
Phone: 833-262-8899

Published by AuthorHouse 12/03/2020

ISBN: 978-1-6655-0999-2 (sc)
ISBN: 978-1-6655-1006-6 (e)

Contents

Introduction

Why write the book?

There is more to life than meets the eye. We see life through our own lenses and viewpoints. Imagine that we are all on a train heading towards one destination. If you are sitting on one side of the train you might see a valley. The people sitting on the other side may only see a wall of mountains. Only the bird up above can see the entire picture. We are all on a journey. *To where?* you might ask. A simple answer that seems to have a consensus is the journey to happiness. Deep down, we all strive for a sense of wellbeing and fulfillment. We believe that if only we had what we really want, we would be happy. Yet, when we attain the object of our desire, sooner, rather than later, that sense of lack returns and so do the thoughts: If only, if only I had what I really want, I would be happy. This pattern of thought is what someone I knew once called "The Cycle of Ignorance."

How do we achieve happiness? Does acquiring material possessions give us long-lasting fulfillment? And the biggest question of all, *why are we here? What is our purpose in life?* Those questions consumed me growing up. And for the longest time, I did not have any answers.

I always felt I was a piece of a puzzle that did not fit into the game of life I was playing. After struggling to find answers for many years, a time came when I had reached the conclusion that life was not worth living. I was close to ending it all and then something unexpected happened that changed my life drastically.

*   *   *

Since my life-changing event, my journey has taken me in various new directions. Each experience has taken on its own form, but the truth revealed by each journey was always the same. What is this truth? That love is the way. Love is the key that unlocks all mysteries. Love is who we are, where we come from, and where we must return. Once we reconnect to that love which is our true nature, we then feel love for our neighbor, and we feel the joy and light that is the essence of this love.

What happens when a ray of sunshine goes through a prism? We see the light of the sun turn into a rainbow. The light is the truth and each color of the rainbow is an expression of the same truth. Just as the light when going through the crystal manifests as different colors, the same applies when truth is revealed in our physical reality. The revelation of truth manifests as different energy vibrations and it appears as different persuasions and paths. Depending on our consciousness, we are attracted to the expression of the vibration that will support our growth.

I have been given numerous experiences that showed me that true power lies beyond our physical reality. These experiences were not drug induced. They were experiences, nevertheless, that shook me to my core and opened my eyes and my heart.

I frequently pondered the thought of why, for many years now, my life has taken me through situations that were not "normal" according to our society. I've had a strong feeling that one of the reasons was that I am meant to share with others what I have lived in this lifetime because many are searching for answers and maybe, just maybe, my answers might resonate with others.

I'm the kind of person that would prefer to hide and not be in the public eye. So, years ago, I wrote a screenplay. My intention was to hide my life experiences behind the scenes created for a fictional movie. My main fear was, *what will people think of me if I express what I have lived through and my unique understanding of my experiences?* I did have some positive feedback with the screenplay but decided to put the screenplay aside.

I have come to realize, now is the time to express what I have lived within my being, regardless of the judgment. It is the time to go beyond my comfort zone and share the journey I have experienced because the result might be that my experiences will help another soul grow and find peace within.

The people involved in my story, regardless of their behavior towards me, were key players in my real-life movie. The roles they played helped in my growth and understanding of life. And for that, I am grateful.

I have changed the names of some of the people and places involved.

In the Beginning

1958

"BABELE, BABELE," I CALLED OUT to my grandma as soon as I got home from school. I knew that she was probably sitting in her room by the window, deep in prayer, with her bible open on her lap. Babele is a Yiddish endearment, a fond word for grandmother. My parents and grandparents left Eastern Europe and fled to Cuba before the Nazis could put their dirty hands on them. In 1939, my grandmother along with my mother, my uncle, and an aunt I never met, were able to leave on the last ship out of Poland. My grandfather and another uncle had left Poland two years earlier to prepare for their arrival. One of my Babele's daughter and grandchildren stayed behind in Poland and were never heard from again.

The Jewish Community in Havana, which was composed mainly of immigrants from Europe, decided to start their own school, *Centro Israelita de Cuba* (Israelite Center of Cuba). They were incredibly supportive of the State of Israel who had only a few years prior, in 1948, become and independent state. In addition to the regular educational curriculum required by law, the school would teach Jewish History and the Yiddish language, which were a significant part of our culture.

1

At school that day, my third-grade teacher told all her students that we were going to start getting ready for our end of the year performance. She informed us the class would be divided into two groups, one group would be performing a ballroom dance with fancy dresses and the other was a performance about the life of the young pioneers living in a Kibbutz in Israel. A kibbutz was a collective community in Israel that was mostly based on agriculture.

"I will let you know tomorrow what roles you will play," the teacher said. I knew immediately that I really did not want the fancy dress, I was meant to be a Pioneer. But, how could I ensure that the teacher would choose me to be a Kibbutznik? Ah, yes, Babele to the rescue! She was always praying. *Could she help me get the part that I wanted? What could I lose if I ask her to put in a good word for me to whoever she was praying all day long?*

As soon as I got home from school, I ran through the house straight into Babele's room. Just as I thought, there she was sitting by her window with her prayer book, her lips silently moving. I waited by the door until she was finished.

My Babele had a difficult childhood. I know she was orphaned at an early age when her parents were killed in a train crash. I do not know much about her childhood besides that, but I can imagine that it must have been very painful. Then later in life escaping Nazi invasion and occupation, and all the horrors that came with it. And as if that were not enough, her youngest daughter, after escaping the Nazis, was murdered in Cuba by her boyfriend.

Her marriage to my grandfather was arranged. What a blessing for them both! My grandfather was a kind, gentle, and loving soul who loved her dearly. He was brought up as a Hassidic Jew but later in life, as my mother would say, "He started reading secular books in secret," which changed his extreme religious beliefs.

2

"Babele, I have something very important to ask you!" I cried. Being a person of very few words, she nodded her head for me to continue. I proceeded to tell her the whole story about the performances at school and how the teacher was going to give us her decision tomorrow. "Babele, please, can you ask God to help me be chosen to be a Pioneer? That's what I really want." She looked at me and gave me a nod yes and a little smile, which was unusual for her because she rarely smiled.

Now, I must tell you how my mother viewed this whole God thing.

My mother, bless her soul, loved, cared for, and respected her mother dearly. Since my grandmother kept kosher and was very observant, my mother always made sure that she had her own refrigerator, plates, and kosher food. Babele never sat at the dinner table with us because we were not kosher but seemed to be content with her daughter's effort to respect her wishes and create an environment that allowed her to follow her own beliefs.

Even though I grew up in a home with a strong Jewish traditional background, when it came to the religion, forget it. Yummy ham was my favorite and who knew about not mixing dairy and meat.

I can still hear and feel my mother's anger and pain when she would say, "How can God exist and allow so many innocent people and children to be murdered?" She was referring to the Holocaust, and my father supported her all the way. I loved my Mami and I loved my Babele and seeing how their love for one another allowed them to hold their own belief, was a blessing. So here I was watching this movie at home growing up and wondering, *is there a God or not?*

I was born with a strong desire to know the purpose of it all. At this stage, the answers to the question about God did not appear. Watching the duality at home had a strong influence on me, and as a result, all I experienced was confusion. The effect of what I witnessed was that I became more of an agnostic. The existence of God became a lingering question I pondered for many years to come.

Oh, in case you are wondering, I did get the Pioneer part. *Hmm…*, my brain thought, *maybe there is a God after all.*

The Sun Begins to Set

1961

"*J*AIME," MY MOTHER CALLED OUT to my father, "make some tilo for Silvia." Used to calm the nerves and aid in sleep, tilo was a tea frequently drank in Cuba.

It was 1961, and the night before my departure from Cuba to the United States. The next morning my mother and father would take me and my cousin Perla to the airport and put us both on a plane to Miami. Lying on my parents' bed crying, I remember being overcome by a fear that I had never felt before. The change from a safe and comfortable life to the unknown was a bit unsettling and earth-shattering to my 12-year-old understanding.

My thirteen-year-old cousin Perla and I, were part of the Jewish version of the Catholic Charities "Operation Peter Pan", a program that ran from 1960 to 1962 and airlifted more than fourteen thousand unaccompanied Cuban children to the U.S. to avoid potential indoctrination by Fidel Castro's Cuban government. By 1960, the Cuban government began reforming education strategies. School children were taught military drills, how to bear arms, and anti-American songs. My mother was at the time working closely with HIAS, the only global

Jewish organization whose mission was to assist refugees. She was involved in getting the permits to the United States for the Cuban Jewish children during this crisis.

The permits were acquired at the US Embassy in Havana. I remember my mother telling me how she hid the American dollars that was going to pay for the permits, in her purse, before entering the embassy. The guard at the embassy searched everyone before entering. If she was caught with American currency, she ran the risk of being arrested. This took courage since this activity was not sanctioned by the Cuban government.

I can hardly imagine what my parents must have been going through. This major change in the stability of our family must have reminded them of their own exile from anti-Semitism in Europe. My seventeen-year-old sister, Felicia, had left Cuba just a few months earlier and was now living with family in Brooklyn, NY. I tried to comfort myself with the thought that I would be seeing my sister soon, along with my aunt, uncle, and cousins who had left Cuba the year before.

My father walked in holding the cup of "tilo" and sweetly encouraged me to drink it. This was the first time I had been offered this special tea, so I knew that my parents were concerned and didn't know what else to do to comfort me. The tea had its intended effect. I quickly fell asleep, got a good night's sleep and was ready in the morning for the next chapter of my twelve-year-old life to begin.

The flight to Miami went smoothly. When we arrived, we were greeted at the airport by a lovely lady representing HIAS. She handled all the paperwork that asked the U.S. Government for political asylum for me and my cousin. I knew little English and she hardly spoke any Spanish. I did know how to say, "thank you very much," which I used repeatedly.

She then took us to her home, fed us and told us that the next day, she would put us on a plane to New York and upon arrival, we would be met at the airport by an American relative that everyone called the "Uncle." This was the first time I became aware that I had an American relative. He was the uncle of my aunt that I was going to be living with in Brooklyn. This uncle turned out to be exceedingly kind, going out of his way to sponsor my whole family's request for asylum to the United States. He was also instrumental in helping my family living in Brooklyn to acclimate to the American society. I remember how he took me to enroll in school and was always available to meet with my teachers. Even years later, he was by my side and acted as a witness when I became an American citizen.

My first night in Brooklyn was memorable but not in a good way. It all started after dinner. My aunt started complaining that my father was a weak man, going on to list a litany of his other traits in a way that was not very flattering. I was stunned because at home, if my parents disagreed or had any complaints about each other, their argument was never done in my presence. To me, my father was the sweetest, kindest man in the world. I did not understand why my aunt was complaining so much about him. My father was a quiet man who adored my mother. He was not aggressive, competitive, or outgoing but a simple man who always put my mother and his family first. In those days, the man was supposed to be the head of the family and in control, but that was not the role my father took on. Instead, my mother was the boss and that worked out just fine. The words I heard coming out of my aunt's mouth were like arrows piercing my heart. After she was done ripping my family to pieces, she announced that "Silvia," not my cousin Perla or anyone else, was going to be the one to wash all the dishes that night. I was in shock and noticed that the whole room became totally silent.

I had just arrived a few hours earlier but instead of feeling welcome, I was made to feel that I was a burden and therefore had to be punished.

So, there I was, standing in front of the sink filled with pots and dishes while my heart sank, and I wondered what I was supposed to do since I had never washed a dish in my life. I was trying to put on a good face and do what I was asked to do, but I could not help but feel a choking feeling of pain and sorrow in my innermost being.

My second night away from my parents, my country, my life, was a rude awakening. The secure and predictable life that I knew growing up in Cuba vanished before my eyes.

Looking back on it now, I understand the difficulties and frustrations that my aunt and uncle endured. They already had to provide for three children of their own. They were in a new country with new customs and language. Living in a small apartment in Brooklyn and now they have two more children to care for, my sister and myself. My cousin Perla was going to be living with her grandmother in another part of town. I am sure that these living arrangements added to my aunt's and uncle's life of insecurity and uncertainty. Who knew when my parents and grandmother would be able to leave Cuba and come and get us?

That night, sleeping next to my sister and cousin, I cried, it seemed like for hours. Finally, the unending sobs exhausted themselves and allowed my body to sleep at least for a bit.

Eventually, my parents would get to the U.S. by going to Jamaica and asking the American Consulate there for political asylum. My father arrived in Brooklyn a couple of months later and then months later, my mother and grandmother followed. At last we were all together which made the hardship of the times an easier issue to overcome.

Lost in a Haze

1967

"AH, LOOK AT ALL THE Lonely People", was the headline in my school's newspaper. I looked at the main picture in the front page and could not believe my eyes. It was a picture of me sitting on the floor with my back against the wall and my forehead resting on my knees. You could barely see my face, but the photographer captured an image of quiet desperation.

It was 1967 and I was a freshman at the City of University of New York. I had just finished pledging for a sorority and my social life was picking up speed. Beatles music was everywhere, and the Vietnam war was in full swing. But I was beginning to feel that it did not matter how many friends or dates I had, something was missing, and I did not fit in. The search for meaning was poking me with a constant tap and the pretense that all was well attempted to cover the cobwebs and silent screams.

I began to dress like a hippie. My hair was very long, and jeans with Indian cotton tops as opposed to skirts and sweaters were my daily attire. I would sit in the Library for extended periods attempting to study and do my assignments but instead I found myself staring into

9

space and daydreaming for hours. My questions about the meaning of life did not subside. *Why did I have to go to school? Why get married and have kids? Why were we alive?* Not understanding the purpose of anything began affecting my studies and enthusiasm to live.

I decided to visit the school counselor hoping she could help me understand why it was so difficult for me to concentrate on my schoolwork. After listening to me express my feelings, she told me that she could not help me, but referred me to the Jewish Family Service agency for further evaluation. The agency provided counseling and support for adults, children and families dealing with a range of issues. The services were provided on a sliding scale which was helpful since my family had only been in the United States for only 5 years since fleeing from Cuba. It was not clear to me why she could not help me, but I was beginning to feel that her impression of what I was going through was serious enough to refer me for therapy.

At the agency, I talked to a therapist who recommended I start group therapy. She told me that there would be others in the group around my age that have similar issues. I started going but I was silent during the sessions and never said a word. I sat there not knowing what to say. I was overcome by an unknown fear and sadness that paralyzed me. After a month of attending the group but unable to share my feelings, they recommended that I have a consultation with their psychiatrist. After the psychiatric evaluation, the psychiatrist asked to speak to my parents about the results of his findings. At the meeting, he told me and my parents and I that if I did not start intense psychotherapy, I would end up in a mental institution. There was an urgency about his statements. I was never told the diagnosis of my "condition" and if my parents knew, they never told me. The times were different.

My parents immediately contacted the psychotherapist that was recommended by the psychiatrist. I began seeing her, initially, three times a week. After a few months, I only needed to see her once a week. My parents covered the cost for the duration of the treatment.

Mrs. Levitt, the psychotherapist, for about eight years, kept me from drowning and ending it all. She extended a life vest while I was treading water. I kept my head above water, sometimes gasping for air, but managed to finish college, get jobs, travel abroad, and have a busy social life with boyfriends and many friends. Even though I did not see a purpose to living, I was able to play the role society had prescribed for me.

The appearance of a normal life hid the continuing nagging questions about what "it" was all about. One of my first memories was receiving a doll for my third birthday. The doll had moving eyes. I was fascinated with the eyes and became totally obsessed with wanting to know what was behind the eyes. I still remember my mother's shock and surprise when she arrived home from work and found the doll without its eyes. I had pulled them out because I needed to know what made them move and what was behind them, so out they came. Fifteen years later, still wanting to know the "why" of it all, but the answers were not forthcoming. I was living a puzzle and my piece did not fit in. I even thought frequently that maybe I should end this crazy movie and commit suicide. I even went as far one day of taking a pair of scissors and scratching my wrists. What stopped me was that I did not want to hurt my parents.

After finishing my sophomore year, I felt the need to get away from it all. I thought that maybe running away from the darkness I was living, would change my life for the better. I later in life realized that you take yourself wherever you go. So, I decided to take some time off from college and live in a kibbutz in Israel. The Six Day War in Israel had just ended and I thought that my parents would approve and be pleased to see me go to Israel and help. My mother was a strong Zionist and throughout the years she helped fundraise in support of the State of Israel. I enrolled in a kibbutz Work-Study Program where I learned Hebrew a few hours a day and then worked in the fields picking fruit, helped in the kitchen and other areas of the kibbutz.

Kibbutz life temporarily eased the desperation imbedded deep within my soul. I shared a room with two American girls my age who were also volunteering. Paula and Patty were sweet and lots of fun to be around. It was a six-month commitment and towards the end of my stay, my roommates and I decided that before leaving, we wanted to visit all the major cities and important sites in Israel. During that time, in 1968, only twenty years after Israel's independence, it was a widespread practice in Israel to hitchhike, so we felt and were told that it would be safe enough for us to stick our thumbs out and just go with the flow.

Travelling with my buddies, Paula and Patty was lots of fun. They were two American girls who also had the desire to come to Israel and experience kibbutz life. We left with our backpacks and excitement for our next adventure.

The kibbutz was in Northern Israel near Nazareth. We headed south, visiting many sites on our way to the southernmost city of Eilat. We were pleased when an Israeli truck driver picked us up to take us on the long drive across the Negev desert to the port city of Eilat. He seemed to be a nice fellow although he didn't speak any English and we spoke a little Hebrew. When we arrived in Eilat, he drove us to the Student Hostel for our stay. Before leaving, he asked me if I wanted to go to dinner with him that night. He seemed nice enough and I thought that it might be fun to have someone show me around town. We decided that he would be back to get me in about an hour.

I remember thinking during my late teens, how trusting and innocent I was. My parents never sat down with me and talked to me about the birds and the bees. I think my mother was a bit embarrassed.

I just did not know what to expect on a date and what to watch out for. The boys I dated in high school and in college, for the most part, were not aggressive and quite respectful. The only sexual education I remember was when I was about twelve years old, right before leaving Cuba, my mother took me to my pediatrician, and he explained to me all about the menstrual cycle. At that time, I still had not experienced menstruation but since my parents did not know when they would see me again, I think that my mother wanted me to be aware of what was coming. That is as far as my parents went in educating me about sexuality and relationships. Those were different times when one did not speak about such things, especially fathers.

I was standing in front of the hostel an hour later looking forward to our date when I saw the truck approaching. I quickly jumped in and off we went. I noticed that he was silent and not responding to anything I was saying. Instead of going in the direction of town, he was going in a different direction. "Where are we going," I asked. No response. I was beginning to become a bit unsettled. He was driving faster and faster away from town. I noticed that we had arrived at the port. It was dark and seemed deserted except for a few docked ships. He found a place to park and opened his glove compartment and there was a gun. He took it and threatened to shoot and throw me in the water where no one would find me if I resisted his sexual demands.

I surrendered but luckily, he was quick. As he drove me back to the hostel, I sat stunned and in shock. What just happened? Was it my fault? We arrived at the Hostel and I quickly got out without looking back. I stood in front of the hostel in total disbelief. What would I tell my waiting friends? I decided to tell them nothing. Well, at least I did not end up with a bullet in my head and dumped in the sea.

That was just the beginning of my experience with sexual assault. On the way back to America, my American kibbutz friends and I decided to travel across Europe. We decided to take a ship from Israel to Greece where we visited Athens and all the major tourist attractions. From Greece, we took a ferry boat to Italy. My minor in college was Art History. What better place to experience major historical artists such as Michelangelo, Da Vinci among others but in Rome, Florence, and other cities in Italy! We had decided to take the train to travel between cities. In Rome, we boarded a train to Florence. Once we had settled into one of the cabins in the train, two conductors came into our cabin, closed the door, and proceeded to attack us. The one who jumped on top of me was twice my size and probably weighed over 200 pounds. He held both of my arms back and because of his weight, he managed to tie me down in such a way that I could not move anything at all. But to his surprise I was able to bite him in the mouth hard. He jumped up in pain and looked at me as if to say, how dare you do this to me? That was the end of that. He walked out never to be seen again.

Maybe because it was during the late 60's and 70's, the time of the sexual revolution, but I could not help but blame myself for these events. I thought, what am I doing to attract such behavior. I felt shame and guilt and could not share it with anyone.

All I really wanted was to travel and experience new places. Having a serious relationship was not on my mind. I can also tell you about the man who was hiding behind a bush who grabbed me while I was walking in the park or the man behind a counter at a store who took my hand and pulled me to the back of the store or the date chasing me at my home and then forcing himself on me.

I did manage, in between the horror of the times, to meet sweet men who were respectful, but the damage had been done and making a commitment did not come easy for me.

Jerusalem

1975

AFTER GRADUATING WITH A B.A. in Psychology, I began working as a childcare worker with autistic and schizophrenic children at Maimonides Institute in Far Rockaway, New York. I worked for about a year and then the owner of the facility offered me a position as a counselor to work for the Residential Treatment Center that he owned in Jerusalem. I was told that he would pay for my fare to Jerusalem and once there, provide room and board. What an opportunity! It was a dream come true. Not only doing the work I felt I was meant to do but in the city of Jerusalem which ignited my heart at a time in my life where emptiness and despair was my constant condition.

It was my first day off from work after arriving in Jerusalem when I decided to visit what was called the Old City. The magic of Jerusalem had me mystified. Some say that it is the energy center of the world. Within the walls of the Old City, the three major religions, Christianity, Judaism, and Islam, attempt to coexist. Walking down the narrow streets of the Arab market, the senses are awakened to cries from the merchants selling their wares and the smell of fresh-brewed Turkish coffee. Old Arab men dressed in their garb sit for hours smoking from

15

their Hookah. My dream to one day live and work in Jerusalem, to be a part of the natural rhythm of life in this fascinating city had come true.

The old Arab market was subdued this lazy morning. The usual cries of the merchants selling their wares and the aroma of Turkish coffee brewing seemed to be on hold. Walking through the old city gates was the door to another time and place. If only the walls could whisper to me its precious secrets. Would it be murder plots finalized, soft caresses from lovers or wisdom from the mouth of unsuspecting men and women? Living in Jerusalem at this time in my life, brought respite from my unanswered questions and at the same time created more confusion about the reasons why I came to be.

While walking through the maze of narrow streets and unexplored territory, I found myself in front of what seemed to be an ancient deserted synagogue in the middle of a square with coffee houses almost touching each side. There was something about this synagogue that had me mesmerized so much so; I did not understand. The old questions returned: *Why are we alive? What is the reason? Is life just about marriage, family, and career? If that is all there was to life, then it was not enough for me, life was of no interest and it did not make any sense. If there is a God, then prove it.*

I ran up the stairs of the coffee shop that had an open terrace, ordered a cup of tea, and became captivated by the historic architecture of the ancient synagogue.

The desire in me to find meaning was strong, a borderline obsession. Although, I always seemed to have good jobs, boyfriends, and friends, but it always felt that there was something missing. The feeling of emptiness and pain was unbearable at times. I was running on empty. The answers never came. As far as I was concerned, it all came to a dead end and that was the option that was frequently weighing heavily on my mind.

It was a windy day in the Old City. The wind carried with it the perfume of the earth, flowers, and trees. A breath of air filled my lungs and the walls began to crumble a bit. I heard the sounds carried by a wind well-travelled. I heard the stormy waves of the faraway sea, the plowing of the earth, the rustling of the trees. I heard my own cry of anguish and laughter diffused with the sounds spread by the wind. *I cling to the wall; it is too high to see. The work is hard, and my strength is running low. I must find my source of energy again. I look within and search for my essence, the infinite truth. The long and winding inward journey begins. The power of the forceful wind leads me through the self-inflicting treacherous hurdles. It is dark. I stumble, fall. Out of my desperate longing I crawl, digging my nails into the void. I cannot afford to stop. It is a matter of survival. While the gentle wind is reassuring and supportive at my side, it carries me onward. Timeless in voyage, the wind is my constant companion. I search and seek, and darkness is all there is. But the wind, the truthful wind, and I are one. The wind is me and I am the wind. And like the wind, I am strong and free.*

Suddenly I realized that it was getting late and I needed to start heading back. I finished my last sip of tea and then rushed through the Old City to the main square to catch a bus back home.

Outside the Old City, the streets were busy with traffic, cars and trucks were honking, people were crossing the streets ignoring the lights. I spotted a restaurant across the street from the bus stop. Thinking that I could get some food to go, I began to cross the street when I saw the bus approaching. I quickly returned and started to push my way to get into the crowded bus. The doors closed but I just managed to get in. The bus drove off while I pushed myself further inside the bus. Suddenly, the bus was rattled by the sound of a loud explosion. *What was that! What just happened?* People inside the bus were screaming and crying but the bus continued its route.

The phone was ringing as I opened the door to my home. A friend from Tel Aviv was calling me to see if I was fine. She told me there had been a terrorist attack at a restaurant in the square outside the Old City. It was the same restaurant I almost visited. I missed the car bomb by minutes. Holding the phone in my hand, I sat there speechless. That was just the beginning of a series of Light and Dark events that I would be experiencing living in Jerusalem.

Working at the Residential Treatment Center for American teens with emotional issues was often very draining. The residents were all struggling with their own negative thoughts, but I remember thinking that the difference between them and me was that they could not control themselves and were quick to act on their impulses. For instant, one night I was supervising in the game room when one of the residents, a young male, walked in, locked the door behind him and pulled out a knife, threatening another young male in the room. I ran and stood in front of him while he was waving his knife. I do not remember what I said to him but after a few minutes, he stopped his tirade, walked to the terrace and climbed down to the lower level. I hurried to the terrace and saw him hiding among the trees and brush. He was found and immediately dealt with. He also received extra attention the weeks that followed. While he was a resident at the facility, he never again expressed any violent behavior towards me or anyone else.

I had an odd incident a few weeks later when a kibbutz friend of mine, Miriam, came to Jerusalem to visit me. We had lunch and then we were going to visit some friends of hers that lived just outside the city. It was a beautiful sunny day, without a cloud in the sky. While we were driving, we reached an area that overlooked the whole city of Jerusalem. The beauty of the Temple Mount was magnificent. The sky was bright blue, but we noticed a solitary cloud perched right above the Old City hovering over the Temple Mount.

We stared at this cloud in astonishment. It looked exactly like Michelangelo's sculpture of "Moses" found in Italy. It was the image of a regal old man, wearing a long white robe, wrapped with a long white undulating beard, sitting on a throne. After a long silent stare, my friend turns to me and says, "If it wasn't for the fact that I don't believe in God, I would say that was God!" I nodded in amazement. Yes, it was only a cloud, the only cloud that the eyes could see, and it was right above one of the holiest places on earth. As a child, I would enjoy looking at the shape of clouds. But this was different. It was alive. I wished that we had stopped the car so we could take in the beauty of the moment a bit longer. But off we went and the sight never to be forgotten.

A couple of weeks after this unusual appearance, I was in my room reading a book on my lunch break when suddenly, the room became translucent and infused with light. I put the book down and became overwhelmed with a feeling of peace while immersed in this calming white light. I looked around and noticed that the walls were not solid anymore. Every molecule had become light and had lost its density. It felt as though I could put my hand through the wall. The density was gone, and everything was light. I then heard a soft and comforting deep male voice resonating through my whole being. It was saying, *"All is well, all is well. I am here, I am here."* I was completely enveloped in a feeling of peace and love that I had never experienced in my life. Every cell in my body was dancing with the essence of this light.

What once felt dead was now full of life. This presence had taken over my empty body and given it life. I sat there stunned, in awe and totally at peace filled with a quiet joy. My experience of what I thought was reality was shattered. Light was shining beyond what seemed to be a veil of illusion. What had just happened? Who or what was this powerful light being that had come to comfort me and lift me out of the drowning darkness? The curtain was lifted, and I was shown a new direction.

I strongly felt the constant gentle presence of this being guiding and showering me with its peace, love, and healing for the next month. The powerful feelings gradually left me, but what remained was the knowledge, awareness and certainty that I was being guided by a loving being who held my hand even during uncertain times and was a constant by my side. The ardent desire to end my meaningless life, a desire I had struggled for years, was completely gone, never to return. A door was opened for me and I entered a new reality, the next phase of my existence.

The following week, I met my friend Miriam for lunch. I had not told her or anyone about my experience. When she saw me, her first reaction was, "You look different!" She went on to say, "You look so at peace and are radiating with Light." I was surprised by her reaction and then told her about my experience.

Shortly after this event, I decided that it was time for me to go back to the U.S. I left Jerusalem with my constant companion by my side, the being that infused me with life. My eyes were now open with a realization there was more to life beyond the physical existence. I had stepped out of a dark cave into a new world, one unfamiliar to me but ready for exploration. I was heading for some unchartered territory. The new search had begun.

New York

1976-77

"SILVIA, PLEASE CALL GOLDA MEIR at her home in Israel and discuss with her the arrangements for her scheduled trip to New York to attend the opening night performance of the Broadway show *Golda*," Joe, my boss, said to me after calling me into his office. The show *Golda* starring Anne Bancroft, was my first assignment as a publicist for one of the top public relations firms in New York City. I cannot tell you how thrilled I was, since after having lived in Israel, I considered Golda Meir, the first female Prime Minister of Israel, one of my heroes.

After leaving Israel, I spent several months in California, first in Santa Cruz and then San Francisco, but New York was calling me. I decided to contact Joe Wolhandler for a job. I had worked with Joe, who was a prominent press agent and publicist in the entertainment field, back in 1973, when he hired me to go on the road to promote the telecast of a Boys Circus from Spain. I heard about this opportunity from a friend, called him and shortly after, I was hired. I left the job after the short stint was over but, but before leaving, Joe said to me that if I ever needed work to call him.

Now three years later, I called Joe and to my surprise, he was quick

21

to remember me and was happy to hear from me. He told me that he was inundated with work and would be incredibly happy to have me work for him again. Coming from California, I had nowhere to stay in New York. Joe graciously arranged for me to live in one of his empty properties, conveniently located close to the office, for a very affordable monthly rate. The property was a furnished brownstone townhome on 72 Street overlooking the East River. It seemed to me as if all the doors were opening for my return to New York.

On my first day back in New York, I decide to explore the area where I would be living and working. I was thrilled to be back in Manhattan. Walking down First Avenue, I felt alive meandering past the pedestrians exploring the abundance of shops and restaurants. One coffee shop I passed seemed out of place, but it caught my attention. The sign on the window said, "GOD is Love" and "GOD Heals." Ever since my life-changing experience in Jerusalem, with "the presence" still at my side, I had been pursuing any knowledge that seemed different from the norm, that might attempt to explain what life is about beyond the physical reality. This seemed to be a coffee house with a Metaphysical twist. I was barely back in New York City eight hours and already I found myself exploring a thought that pulled me, "God Heals." *What kind of a place is this? What are they all about?*

Back when I was living in San Francisco, I was introduced to numerology, which fascinated me. I remember spending hours over coffee discussing numbers, their meaning and interpretations with a fellow numerologist. I had just about every book on the subject available at the time. I studied it and could use it to accurately describe people's personalities. The day before leaving San Francisco for New York, I decided to attend a Psychic Fair at the Metaphysical Foundation. I was drawn to a middle-aged lady with wavy red hair. This was the first time I interacted with a so called highly intuitive woman. The first thing she said to me was that I had to go back to New York to meet the person who would become my spiritual teacher. She also said that the job offer was a way to get me to New York to meet a group of people who were part of a strange religion. She saw them lined up and laying their hands-on people for healing. I was returning to New York because of them. She went into some detail that at the time didn't make sense to me but later proved to be true. So, when I saw the sign on the coffee shop, it piqued my curiosity and I decided to go in, explore this God heals thing and have some coffee.

I was greeted by a gorgeous man in a blue suit with an Irish accent who called himself Father Luke. The place was not crowded at all, except for a couple of men and women wearing blue with a chain around their necks that had a strange symbol hanging from it. They all began their names with either Father, Mother, Brother or Sister. To my astonishment, the people running the coffee shop were all beautiful, friendly and very bright. I felt puzzled, as to why such handsome and intelligent people be wearing what seemed to be a uniform and calling themselves Mother this and Father that. My mind could not process this. These are the kind of people that you would see climbing up the ladder of corporate success and stardom. This disconnect aroused my curiosity even more which pushed me for further exploration. What is it about this place that attracted such powerful, intelligent beings that did not seem to fit with how the rest of the world functioned? From our conversation, I gathered that the God they were describing was a Universal and Non-Denominational God which I found pleasing. The organization was called "God Heals Foundation."

As a Jew born in Cuba, I did not identify with a name for God and was not brought up even believing in any God because of my mother's painful memories regarding the Holocaust. I was taught that I was a Jew by birth regardless of whether I believed in God or not. The Jews in Cuba created their own close-knit community by sending their children to a school that taught the Yiddish language and building a Temple where the holidays were celebrated. Despite my grandmother's total devotion and faith, I was a cultural and traditional Jew not a religious one.

Cuba was a Catholic country. My memories of Jesus growing up in Cuba were the many images of Christ with a crown of thorn on his head and blood dripping down his face that were found in every home and place of worship. As a child, it was a little scary for me to look at the dripping blood. I also did not understand what all the different statutes meant, was never taught about it, and did not want to know. So, I was a bit more open to listening about a universal God that was loving, could heal and didn't belong to one religion.

After my first interaction with the people at the coffee house, I was invited to attend their "Healing Celebration" that was held every Saturday night. I came back the following Saturday to see what this Healing Celebration was all about. When I entered their assembly room, calming, soothing music was playing, setting the mood, and creating an atmosphere of peace that quieted my fast beating- heart.

The room was filling up quickly and soon we were all told to take our seats because the program was about to begin. To my surprise, Father Luke walked in, guitar in hand, followed by two others who took their place at the piano and bass. They began playing while Father Luke sang repeatedly, "*We come from the Light and to the Light we must return. We come from the One and to the One we must return. Guided by the Light, Guided by the One.*"

Not only was this man gorgeous, but his voice and music were able to quiet our conscious minds and take us to another place where the heart led. At that moment, someone asked if anyone in the audience needed healing to come up to the stage. Several people went to the stage and formed a line. Shortly after, men and women wearing blue stood behind the people asking for healing and laid their hands on their shoulders.

The music continued but I was totally blown away. *Isn't this what that psychic in San Francisco, just a few days before, saw as the reason I had to return to New York? What just happened? What is this all about?* A strange prediction coming true in such a short time. I did not know then, but I had just entered a universe that was in the world but not of it, a Universe that would become my life for the next thirteen years.

Clashing of Two Worlds

$\mathscr{I}$ BEGAN FREQUENTING THE COFFEE HOUSE after work and began experiencing a world whose focus was a desire to heal, help others, foster spiritual growth, and assist in transformation. At the same time, I began spending time in a completely different world where importance and value was given to celebrities, movie stars, the image of grandeur, and the possession of things.

From the moment I called Golda Meir at her home in Israel, I became totally immersed with an experience which many dream about, but I was living it. Once Golda arrived in New York City, my days were spent promoting the show. Who can forget the time I found myself taking Golda to meet the Mayor of New York City where she was given the "Keys to the City" and later interrupting a press conference between Golda and the Governor of New York because it was time to take her to the opening night of the Broadway show *Golda*. How often does one get the opportunity to stop traffic in Manhattan while riding in one of the limousines that is being escorted, sirens screaming, by the New York police?

Once the play premiered, I spent every night before the show in Anne Bancroft's dressing room while the makeup artist was transforming her into Golda Meir. I was there to intervene if members of the press decided to intrude without an appointment and then stayed after the show when many celebrities came backstage after the performance to wish her well.

Even though I was enjoying every bit of it, at the same time, I seemed to be observing the experience from a different viewpoint. I remember the time, it was in 1977, when I was the publicist for the telecast of the Miss Universe and Miss USA Pageant. I was invited to bring Miss USA to Studio 54, the *in place* at the time, for the opening night party of the movie *Grease*. After getting out of the limousine, we were rushed in past hundreds of bystanders waiting to get a glimpse of a celebrity. The man at the entrance didn't even ask for our invitation. We were part of the *in-crowd*, the pretty people, the *famous*. Inside, the disco was filling up. The décor was 50s, *Grease*-era style.

I released Miss USA to mingle with the crowd while I wandered around exploring. My first stop was where a group of people was gathered around a lady posing against a 50s Chevy. Was she breathing? She was stiff and lifeless. It was "Art," I was told. Looking closely, I noticed that it was Diane Von Furstenberg posing as a mannequin with a group of about five men surrounding her. I recognized a couple of the men. They had major roles in the Broadway show *Hair*. All the men were gabbing away while Ms. Furstenberg stood still, without flinching an eyebrow. At the same time, Olivia Newton-John, the guest of honor, star of *Grease* was dancing away, while John Travolta was celebrating the opening night of *Grease* in Los Angeles.

After chatting with many people including a world-famous pianist and the handsome Ed Byrnes, who starred in the hit 60s TV show *77 Sunset Strip*, I meandered away from the increasing crowd and noise. I needed space. The disco was in a large warehouse, but I was beginning to gasp for air. The music seemed to be getting louder and louder. The cigarette smoke was beginning to burn my eyes. The flashing lights and loud music were deafening. I needed to get away, but where was Miss USA? I couldn't leave without her. I found stairs that went up to the balcony. To my surprise, the balcony was empty. I was standing alone on the balcony watching the crowd. What a sight! All I saw were a few hundred people screaming their pain. They thought that they were having fun. I had a vision of beyond. The illusion of the physical reality was lifted and what was left was loneliness, fear, and excruciating pain hiding behind the masquerade of being the desired privileged, supposedly having fun. This façade had a crack and I saw the reality beyond the image. It became very unattractive.

I believed my Guide was there showing me another situation devoid of light. It was all an illusion. I began to feel compassion for the pain these beings were feeling. Lost in the lie, drowning in darkness. When the light shines, one can see the truth and the truth can be painful but offers freedom from being enslaved by lies. When true vision is restored, with the help of the light, it makes choosing so much easier. Choose death living a lie in darkness or choose life with the light. The choice seemed to be simple. Life with the light.

So many people wanted to be in my position, to be a part of the *in -crowd*. But all I could think of was the joy and peace and presence of life that I felt every time I went to the "Coffee House," and visited a group of people that exuded a beauty and a spirit I recognized from many moons ago.

Decision Time

1978

UPON MY RETURN FROM ACAPULCO, after spending a month promoting the Miss Universe Pageant in Mexico, I made my final decision to become part of the God Heals Foundation. It was less a decision than an urgency to dive into the unknown sea of what I knew would be answers.

The "Presence" I felt as my constant companion would quietly and softly bring to my awareness that truth would be found with total commitment and abandonment to the path laid before me. I basically didn't have a choice. It was either continue living the illusion of this realm devoid of any nourishing light or step into the unknown with a full trust of the divine. What a paradox! If I stayed in my present position, what appeared to be a successful press agent, working with the "Rich and Famous," would bring death to my soul. But if I gave up my position in life, which was desirable to many, and allowed to be ridiculed for being associated with what "seemed" to be an obscure group, I would be given life. I had come to one of the major crossroads of my young life. I saw one road lead to darkness, the other to the light.

At that time, I told the man I was dating my decision to give up everything and see where this path would lead me. He was silent as I shared my conviction. After a few minutes, he asked me if before joining the group, I could meet him one more time. He wanted to take me to a secret gathering, by invitation only, to learn about the ancient Jewish wisdom called Kabbalah. This was in 1978 and the study of Kabbalah was something I had never heard of but was open to see what it was all about.

We went to an apartment in Manhattan. When we arrived, the room was dimly lit and there were about fifteen people sitting in a circle studying from an ancient text. My friend and I joined the circle while one of the people read from the ancient text and translated its meaning and significance. The study lasted more than an hour. I found it interesting but at that time it was not pulling me. Little did I know then that almost twenty years later, Kabbalah would become a major lifeline in my life. I thanked my date for introducing me to Kabbalah, but I told him that I felt a strong calling to dive into the path of the God Heals Foundation.

I then quit my job, gave up my apartment and my possessions. To become part of the community, I had to take a vow of celibacy and poverty. They provided a place to live and food, plus a $25 a week allowance. All I had left were some clothes and a sleeping bag. I did hold on to a camel hair coat. To me it was a symbol of the life I was just releasing. Ironically, not too long afterwards, the coat was stolen by a homeless person in the street. I am sure that he needed it more than me.

My friends and family were shocked. Years later, I was told by friends that they were planning to come and rescue me from the group. My decision was not based on following a guru or ideology, but it was knowing that my own internal compass was guiding me to a destination that would bring answers.

It was early fall in Manhattan. A new adventure was ahead. If only I had known what really lay before me.

One evening, shortly after I made the commitment, I arrived at the coffee house for my regular duties and was informed that David, one of the original and most senior members, had come for a visit to share a very important message with the group. Everyone seemed to be very excited and started to get the place ready for what seemed to be a very important meeting. I had never met David or even heard about him. I asked a few questions and was told that he was Jewish, one of a handful Jews that were part of the organization. By then, they all knew that I was also a Jew.

We had all gathered in the assembly room. David, a handsome, red-headed Englishman, cheerfully greeted all in his path as he made his way to the front of the room. Once he was seated, the room became silent.

He began by explaining how certain events in the organization's journey had changed the direction of its path and what he would reveal to everyone that day would take them in a different direction; one which would add to their experience and knowledge.

As a group, the organization believed they were guided through what they called "Enactments," another word for role playing and acting something out, in order to live and learn firsthand what life was all about. They had lived through these "Enactments" in the past, and as a result, they changed their belief systems to experience firsthand and acquire the knowledge required for their spiritual growth.

With great authority, David announced he recently had a very powerful vision. A presence appeared to him. He was in his room and it lit up with a great white light. Everything became light and he was infused with an overwhelming feeling of peace. He then heard a voice saying to him, "Peace be with You." He continued describing what happened to him and all I could think of was the immense similarity of his vision to what I had experienced in Jerusalem. I had never shared

33

with anyone in the organization the life-altering experience that I had in Jerusalem. No one knew. The coincidence was mind blowing to me. The only difference was that he called it Jesus! He went on to say that it was a sign that from that moment on, we would all become Christians. Suddenly, the silence in the room burst into cries with people saying, "Thank you Jesus, Thank you Jesus."

Waves of shock ran through my body. Not Jesus Christ! It couldn't be. Please, let it not be Jesus. I couldn't believe my ears. I am a Jew, not a Christian. To become a Christian and follower of Jesus Christ was the unthinkable. What had I gotten myself into! I had committed myself to a non-denominational group, not Christianity. I felt certain that my Guide, my constant companion, led me to this situation, but I couldn't help feeling double-crossed.

In total disbelief, sobbing uncontrollably, my heart pounding, I stormed out of the coffee house, into the night. I heard someone in the distance asking me to come back and talk about what had happened. I didn't look back. I found myself walking the streets of Manhattan, late at night, hysterically crying. This was so unlike my calm, serene way of dealing with unexpected events. I couldn't suppress my feelings. It was more like an outpouring of grief and pain. I couldn't comprehend my extreme reaction to the news. I could not stop crying. It didn't make sense.

I got home, still crying. I dropped everything and jumped into bed, my eyes red and swollen. As I closed my eyes, a strange thing happened. Very vividly, I saw a tall cross with a man nailed to it. A woman dressed in black, kneeling at the foot of the cross, bent over, crying in deep sorrow over the event facing her. The woman's grief was very deep and in direct measure to the all-encompassing love she was feeling for the man on the cross. As I watched this scene in my mind's eye, I saw a powerful bright light emanating from the man on the cross. He was intentionally projecting himself and his light in the direction of this woman. This energy and light enveloped the sorrowful woman and her tears stopped.

She raised her head and longingly looked at the man on the cross. Her brightness revealed their powerful connection. At this point, a total peace came over me. A warm, loving, compassionate and comforting feeling enveloped me. I suddenly realized that the light coming from the man on the cross, was the same Presence and light that had appeared to me in Jerusalem. *Could it be that they were one and the same?* I felt the connection and knew it in my heart instantly. I now understood the pain that I had been feeling. It was a deep and long-forgotten memory that had rekindled at the mention of Jesus Christ. I knew him then; and he is with me now. He touched and healed the pain then and now. I gently drifted into a deep and peaceful sleep with a new understanding.

The Lake House

1978

"BRING A TOWEL, A SLEEPING bag, and a change of clothes," we were told. "Tomorrow, we are all going to be baptized." The location remained a mystery. As a newcomer at the bottom of the hierarchy of the God Heals Foundation, I was not privy to much information about the journey.

At the first sign of dawn, we all got into various cars and vans. By the route we were taking, it became apparent that we were heading in the direction of Westchester, a town north of Manhattan.

As I looked out the car window, seeing the city landscape slowly disappear, I silently wondered whether I should reveal that I was totally ignorant as to what "getting baptized" was all about. I had heard the term before but didn't have a clue as to what it entailed. It was probably my sheltered Jewish upbringing that kept me from being exposed to what it meant. But after thoughtful consideration, I gathered enough courage to ask the question. "Why are we going to get baptized? What does it mean? How does it work?" The people in the car eyed each other but patiently explained the history of baptism and its significance. I explained to them how throughout my whole life

I never wanted anything to do with Jesus and Christianity because I found being constantly exposed in Cuba to statues of Jesus covered in blood unbearable. This strong emotional reaction created in me a feeling of avoidance of Jesus and Christianity.

So why, I asked myself, not just say "Bye, bye, this is not for me!" Simple. But my famished hunger to know the "why" of all that is, the certainty that I was being guided, and that this path would reveal pieces of the puzzle along the way, sustained me on course. I had stepped into a drama unfolding, was now a participant in a theatrical play where the characters improvised and allowed themselves to be led by an unseen director calling the shots behind a veil of mystery. "We are going through a Christian enactment," I kept on hearing. "We learn by putting ourselves in the way of the light and by allowing ourselves to be led. When we take a step back, we can see an enactment of a real-life play and are then able to dissect the drama. Our spiritual growth comes from the knowledge we gain because of these enactments. As an organization, we have gone through various enactments in the past. Now, we are being guided to become Christians. Every cell of our being is ignited with a passion to play a part in the game. Trust that the light has you on this journey which eventually you will understand. The light is not through with you yet!"

The sky was overcast as we pulled up in front of a large, well-manicured New England style house by a lake. An inch of snow had fallen overnight and the thermostat hanging showed a mere fourteen degrees. The house belonged to the organization. I was told that it was used as their retreat.

As we entered the house, we were each told about our overnight accommodations and instructed to assemble by the lake in thirty minutes. Glass doors and large windows covered the side of the house overlooking the lake. The glass doors opened to an expansive deck.

The view was breathtaking. The lake was huge, circled halfway by mountains.

The sun that morning was attempting to peek, leaving a slight glare on the thin ice now covering the surface of the lake. I could not believe that we were all going to be totally submerged in the freezing water. From the house, we walked downhill to the shore. The three most senior members went in first, breaking the ice as they entered the water. They said a prayer and quickly started calling people to come in, three at a time. One after another, participants were pushed down below the frigid lake water in the name of Jesus Christ.

Finally, my turn came. I rushed in and it was over in a matter of seconds. As soon as I stepped out of the ice water, I was overcome by an uncontrollable feeling of joy and laughter. While climbing up the hill to the house, freezing and dripping wet, the muscles in my stomach vibrated with songs of laughter. As the sounds of the laughter reverberated, I felt lighter than air.

Back in my room, I put on some dry, warm clothes and then headed back out to the deck overlooking the lake and the mountains. The beauty of the scenery had intensified one hundred-fold. As I watched, mesmerized by the snow-covered mountains in the background, I heard the mountains roar with laughter, then the sky, the lake and even the air roared louder in response. In an instant, I heard it all become One. What I heard was the deep, compassionate laughter of the One, expressing magnificent pleasure and love as a Father has for His children. The Father taking pleasure at the love His children were expressing for Him and great love for the lengths we went to please Him. I stood overwhelmed by a feeling of joy, becoming one with the One.

Evening came and we gathered around the fireplace. After a couple of people recounted the events of the day, we were guided into a meditation to reflect on what we needed to let go to become pure channels of the light.

During the meditation, it became clear to me that my biggest obstacle was myself, my ego, my selfish desires, my self-absorption. I prayed with all my heart for God, the light, to tear the "I" away from me, no matter what it took. My desire to tear my ego apart became very strong. I became aware of how that was the thick curtain that prevented the light from shining from my soul and to my being. It was so clear to me that a transformation needed to take place. I needed to transform from a "me" oriented being to one whose only orientation and desire was to bring light to the world.

Little did I know then that what awaited me was the fulfillment of this desire made available by a cast of characters playing their appointed roles.

Morning came and we were ready to head back to the city. One of the senior members stood by the front door, laid her hands on our heads and blessed each one of us as we were leaving. While I was waiting to receive a blessing, I noticed that the people already outside were pointing to the sky with an expression of awe and wonder. What could be happening outside? My curiosity expanded as I saw everyone, once outside, in total disbelief. As I walked out, my eyes immediately looked up to the sky searching. It was a sunny day, bright blue sky, not a cloud in the sky. Right above the house, in the sky, was a small upside-down rainbow. I had never in my life seen anything like it. It was the smile of the One on High shining colorfully upon us.

Texas

1979

*S*OON AFTER THE CHRISTIAN PATH was established, major changes began occurring within the organization and among us individually. The first one which affected me the most was the decision to close the coffee house in Manhattan and begin ministries in other parts of the country. I was told that I would be going to Texas to help start a "Clown Ministry," a program of entertainment for hospitalized children. I would be traveling in a van, first to Houston and then Dallas with Peter and Matt, two senior members of the organization. Since we were Christian ministers, I was also told that it was a custom to change our name and adopt the name of a Biblical person. I chose the name Hannah who was the mother of Samuel found in the Old Testament. We had all taken a vow of poverty but also celibacy. This was fine with me considering my history of having been a victim of sexual exploitation. I felt safe, trusted and looked forward to spending time with Peter and Matt.

We arrived in Houston late one night. One of their friends that lived in Houston, had invited us to stay at their house for a few days but since we arrived too late, we decided to sleep in the van and wait until the next day to contact the friends. In the meantime, we parked in an empty parking lot next to a business building and decided to call it a night.

We were awakened in the middle of the night by loud banging and the alarming sound of men yelling, "Open up, this is the police, open up!" Half asleep and fully clothed, we opened the van doors to find three policemen pointing rifles at us and ready to shoot. Who knows what they were expecting but once they looked at us and we explained to them that we were ministers, they put their rifles down but very sternly commanded us to leave the area because we were illegally parked. *Welcome to Texas!*

In the morning, we settled into our temporary accommodations. We were told that we could not use the kitchen, had to sleep on the floor or couch and if we wanted to take a shower, there was no hot water. I wasn't accustomed to such spartan accommodations but hey, I was young and felt ready for the adventure!

Shortly after we settled in Peter told me that since we had no money, the only way that we were going to manage our immediate and organizations' needs was to ask for donations. This was done by going to a commercial street in town with a can in hand and approaching people walking by to ask them for money. That morning, we went to a busy downtown area and stood on the sidewalk in front of a department store. Peter handed me a can and told me to start asking people for donations for our ministry. It didn't take me very long to get the hang of it and I did well for a newbie. Besides asking for cash donations, we got pretty good at going to McDonald's and asking for food donations. Who knew that in Texas at that time, McDonald's gave a free burger and fries to ministers who were working for the Lord? We ended up eating lots of cheap McDonald's hamburgers. Not very healthy but who's asking when you are hungry?

After our first day in Houston and many hours of pounding the streets, we returned to our very modest accommodations. I was a bit tired from all the walking but felt a sense of accomplishment by the end of the day. I managed to collect quite a bunch of change and dollar bills for the cause.

Back home, I noticed that Peter and Matt were gone so I decided to relax and watch a bit of TV. I turned on the TV and sat on the couch ready to let go of the day.

Not long after sitting, I suddenly find myself looking at myself from above. I saw my body sitting on the couch from the vantage point of the ceiling. I felt a deep sense of freedom from not being attached to a body and being pulled down by gravity. I was weightless and felt a profound sense of liberation from the physical. I continued flying away and found myself in a place where I heard a voice tell me, "It's not your time yet! You must go back! You still have much to do!" I did not want to return because it felt so good and free, wherever I was, but suddenly, I was back in my body in front of the TV. Bewildered, I asked myself, *what just happened! Here we go again. Another otherworldly experience to add to my list.*

Years later, I came across a description of what they called an out-of-body experience: "a vivid feeling of being detached from one's body, usually involving observing it and its environment from nearby or above." It seemed to fit my experience to a tee. Another powerful and unforgettable moment to remember.

The following morning, we left for another day of pounding the streets for donations. I didn't tell Matt or Peter about my unusual experience the previous night. I was still processing the event and wasn't ready to share it. While we were walking down the street on the way to the car, I tripped over a crack on the sidewalk and found myself falling. I started falling but the sensation was of an invisible force under me breaking my fall. Peter and Matt both looked at me and said, "I had never seen anyone fall in slow motion." It did feel as if invisible hands intercepted me and placed me on the sidewalk very gently. Yet another strange occurrence, this time going against gravity in this physical reality.

These tiny cracks in the physical reality allowed me to see, experience, and realize that there is another world that coexists alongside this physical world, another world of light.

Little did I know then that the powerful memories of these rays of light would be my life support from the darkness that I was about to enter.

Dallas, Texas

1979

"LET'S SHRED HANNAH!" I HEARD someone say while I was trying to fall asleep. My heart skipped a beat when I heard the enthusiasm that resonated behind those words. We had recently arrived in Dallas to start our Clown Ministry. Peter's wife and others had rented a house and were waiting for us to start our next phase in our spiritual journey. Since I was the junior member, I was left out of their meetings and decision making. It was unanimous, it was Hannah's turn to have her ego demolished. Wasn't that what I had begged for in my silent prayers? Well here we go. The answer to my prayers.

One of the first signs of what was waiting for me was the time that I was walking down the stairs in the house where we lived and passed Matt on his way up. He stopped me, stared at me, his eyes filled with hatred and then he said to me, "I know who you really are" as his piercing eyes threw daggers into my sinking heart. How unusual for Matt to talk to me that way. He was always sweet and friendly. This private interaction was very much out of character. *What was that all about?*

Gradually, I began to feel as if I lived in a fog. The otherworldly moments and experiences that had lifted me quickly disappeared and were replaced by a sensation of having entered a black hole that was swallowing me alive. At times, I didn't ever hear people talk to me. They sounded far away.

Very soon, I learned that "the community" was enacting a time when the Jews of the organization were being scrutinized. The spotlight was on the Jews, seen through the eyes of people who believed that the Aryan race was supreme. Was this part of the Christian Enactment or maybe we should call it the Jewish Enactment? This time, they believed that the Jews were evil, and they were about to prove it. So, anything that went wrong within the organization was the Jews' fault. There was a total of four Jews that were part of the group and I was one of them.

Throughout my life, I heard a lot about anti-Semitism and hatred towards the Jews. In Cuba, we had a close-knit Jewish community. I personally, until the age of twelve when I left Cuba, never felt any hatred directed at us by the Cubans for being Jewish. New York was a melting pot of different cultures and religions. I always felt welcomed by my sweet Italian friends and never felt discriminated against because of being Jewish. This does not mean that there was not an underlying mistrust and hatred towards the Jews. I personally was not exposed to it.

I can only remember one time when I was working as a secretary in the Spanish and Portuguese Department of New York University while I was finishing my last year of college. The head of the department, one of the professors and I were chatting. They started bad mouthing some Jews and saying some horrendous things about them. I thought that since they knew I was from Cuba, they assumed that I was not Jewish and felt comfortable saying negative generalizations about the Jews. I kept my mouth shut because first, I was shocked at their behavior and second, I was frightened to say anything. So, in general, I was not constantly inundated and attacked by others with anti-Jewish sentiment.

It all changed after I made a commitment to this community in order to find out what life was all about and what lies beyond.

My saving grace during my years with this community was that I was good at fundraising. I would go out with my can, go downtown, and stand in front of a busy store. I asked people to help our ministry which included a program of entertainment for hospitalized children. The response was positive. I would bring home at times close to one hundred dollars in donations. This was considered substantial at the time. Besides my daily contribution of cash, I became quite skilled at making calls to businesses and requesting donations of toys and other items that were needed for our work in Dallas.

The Clown Ministry got off the ground with a bang. We visited hospitalized children and brought them music and joy. I became known as "Poppy the Clown" and appeared on various radio and TV shows promoting the work that we did with the children. Despite it all, I was still the Jew who was the source of evil.

I started getting regular calls from one of the most senior members of the community. He would spend close to an hour asking me questions about my life and how I felt about various issues. The truth is, I do not remember specifically what he wanted to know. It felt as if he wanted information that was probably related to whatever they were pursuing regarding this "Jewish Enactment." All I can remember is that he was interested in what I had to say and was never rude or hateful. It seemed to me that he really wanted to know me and keenly listened to whatever I had to say. I enjoyed talking to him on the phone and felt a strong connection. He lived in another state, but I began to look forward to our phone conversations. Something he said one time to the group has stuck with me till this day and it is, "Love is wanting to know." His wanting to know about me, for whatever reason, did create a feeling in me of caring whether that was his intention or not.

One night, when we were deep into the "Jewish Enactment," and right before falling asleep, I experienced a vision/dream that helped me clarify my involvement in my current situation. In this semi-dream state, I was a German woman married to a high-ranking Nazi. Personally, I did not harbor any hatred towards the Jews or felt that they were any less. I found what was happening in Germany appalling and the atrocities inconceivable. But because of my lack of courage, I kept my mouth shut and went along with it. This vision made it clear that my current experience as a Jew in an environment that portraited the Jews as evil and blamed them for anything that went wrong was necessary for my growth. I was living the pain and injustice that I had allowed to perpetrate at a different time through my silence and passive acceptance.

It is very real to me now that we have lived many lives. When one is limited to the illusion of the five senses, one is blind to the different realities that exist simultaneously and is not able to see beyond the physical reality. The people in the group who believed that they were superior because of their race, did not seem to be aware that their soul had lived many lifetimes in diverse bodies and each time, it lived through different experiences in order to reach a point of Oneness with the Light that only knows love.

Believing that you are better because of the color of your skin, how much money you have, how elevated spiritually you think you are or any other excuse for self-aggrandizement, creates a duality which manifests in the feeling of separation, fear and hatred. This feeding of the ego was exactly the opposite of what the community was preaching. I suspect that we all have our own lessons to learn and the community was learning theirs.

Dallas was not all that dark after all. Enter another life changer for me. Soon after I arrived in Dallas, I was given the gift of a dog. I never had a pet in my life and as a child I feared dogs. One day, I got home after a long day fundraising. I walked in and found a small furry creature wagging his tail. I was presented with a gift. "This is for you. He was rescued from a bad situation and needs a good home and we thought that you could take good care of him," I was told. "But," I say, "I don't know the first thing about taking care of a dog."

"Don't worry", I was told, "you will learn. We are here to support you.'" The founders of the community had a great fondness for animals. They would always say that animals were God's innocent creation. Most of them had rescued many dogs and cats. Some even built special home extensions to provide a happy and healthy space for their cats. Their animals were such a priority that they even arranged their living conditions to accommodate their pets.

So, here I was faced with a small black puppy. The first thing I did was give him a name, "The Great Santini," Santini for short, naming him for a character in a novel by Pat Conroy. That was the beginning of my love affair with dogs and my development of an understanding and compassion for animals. They give us so much more than we can ever give them. They teach us unconditional love. They teach us how to give to others without an agenda. I will always be eternally grateful to this community for opening my heart to the love of animals.

Red Rock Retreat

1984

AFTER DALLAS, I WAS SENT to other cities to start Clown Ministries and raise funds for our work. While I was busy focusing on my daily challenges, I heard that the community had decided to buy a large piece of land to start an animal sanctuary for homeless and abused pets. It made a lot of sense since the love of animals was at the heart of the people in this community.

After many months of searching, they found a piece of land in Arizona around 3,000 acres. The place was majestic. It was near the Grand Canyon in Red Rock country. This was virgin land, practically uninhabited. In the 20th century, it was used by the movie industry to film some westerns. This was the land where the Anasazi Indian called home until the 13th century when the Anasazi people suddenly disappeared. There are a few theories as to why they disappeared, but no one knows exactly why. The Hopi Indians claim that they are a descended from the Anasazi. After acquiring the land, the senior members of the community decided to call this piece of land "Red Rock Retreat."

I was living in Colorado at the time and I was informed that I would be driving a truck with building materials and other items, to the retreat. Tim, one of the original founders of the organization, who was also an architect, was living on a trailer and was anxiously waiting for the materials he needed to start the construction.

I had never driven a truck and had little experience driving a stick shift. This was an eighteen-foot truck that I had to drive from Colorado through the Rocky Mountains to Arizona. Two other people came along, but I was the one assigned to drive. Why me? Who knows? It was a bit unsettling, but I managed to get to Red Rock retreat in one piece.

As soon as I set foot on the land, I was awestruck by the beauty of the landscape. The innocence of nature intertwined with the busting colors of the rocks had me transported to another world. I now understood why it was called "The Red Rock Retreat." Once entering this land, one entered a dimension where peace and tranquility coexisted.

The following day, we decided to explore the land.

The following is an article I wrote for the community's publication in 1990 describing my experience **"On First Visiting Red Rock Retreat."**

A visit to the caves

The first time I visited Red Rock Retreat, when Tim was living up there alone in the middle of winter with Bertie Basset Hound, Don, Erin, and I took a tour of the land. We went across the creek to a series of three Indian caves. One of the caves had little black handprints on the walls. The place had an otherworldly feeling to it. I had a desire to walk away alone and sit for a bit and allow the place to absorb me. It was February, and I found a place with lots of tiny dried flowers. I sat and became fascinated by a single square foot of land. All the tiny rocks and flowers... It seemed to be a world within a world.

Suddenly, something very odd and frightening happened. I felt transported to another dimension. I was sitting on a rock that was about a hundred feet from the caves when everything became light and translucent. Nothing was solid. All was light and energy. No separation. Everything was one and connected. I became a part of the All and felt a tremendous amount of power available to make things change and alter with thought. I had the power, if I wanted it, to change everything in an instant. A power beyond the corrupt human power that enslaves.

Reality and Illusion

I realized that this *was* reality: the real essence, not the illusion that we are living. It frightened me in the moment because I did not know what to do with all that power. It had come in an instant and it lasted seconds but the awareness and knowledge that came with it has been with me since. I remember wishing that I could learn to use that power and be more in control of it. But who would teach me? I remember feeling disappointed because I thought it would never happen. But I am beginning to think that it will indeed happen, and perhaps soon, and that the element that will make it all possible is love.

Awakening

What it all meant to me was that we have been asleep for eons. Living in a hypnotic trance. Believing that we are our bodies, that what surrounds us on this plane is reality, and all the things we are told to believe is the only truth. But what is changing is our awareness of who we really are. What is emerging is a recognition of our angelic nature.

We are formed from the light. The light is God, and God is love.

* * *

The Next and Final Stop

Las Vegas
1985

*I*T WAS 1985, AND THE next major project for our community would be to build an animal sanctuary at Red Rock retreat. Las Vegas was only a few hours away from Arizona and it was decided to start a ministry in Las Vegas to help in the building of what was going to be later called "Four Paws Animal Retreat."

One evening, I was invited to attend a gathering for some of the members of the community to be held at the retreat. At that time, there were already some people who were involved in the building of the animal sanctuary housed up there. I was thrilled to be returning to such an enchanted land where, on my first visit, I had been unexpectedly transported by experiencing the illuminating light that exists simultaneously within our being.

Some days later, I arrived late in the afternoon just before sundown. The rays of the waning sun sparkled against the red rocks of the desert landscape. A feeling of peace overwhelmed me as I entered the sandy roads of this magical place.

That night, I joined about twenty of the community members, some

I had not seen in a while, who had traveled many miles to come together to celebrate this new path in our spiritual journey. After dinner, we built a bonfire amongst the red rocks and under the star-filled sky and silence of the night. Gradually, we could hear the crackling of the flames as the fire grew larger and larger. We started by holding hands and forming a circle around the fire in prayer. Soon after, the drums were brought out, we all started singing and dancing around the fire. The energy was so powerful, I felt as if the Anasazi Indians, who once occupied this land 500 years before, had joined us in this powerful celebration of the land and its magic.

Following what felt like a love ceremony to the Earth and the Universe, I felt totally cleansed and at peace. We all sat together and went into a meditative state and were told to ask the Universe to tell us what we needed to know. At that moment, I heard loud and clear with certainty and a total knowing, "Joy!" Nothing seemed more important than to reach a level of joy in this lifetime. But how does one reach such a level living in this physical reality that contains so much pain, suffering and judgment?

While I was sitting enveloped in a meditative state after the powerful celebration around the fire, I looked to my left and noticed that sitting next to me was one of the community members I always tried to avoid. I always felt uncomfortable around him. But this time it was different.

I looked at him and all I felt was unconditional love. My judgment and negativity were nonexistent in that moment. How could I not see anything wrong with him? All I felt and experienced was love for him. No duality. No separation. I knew that we were all interconnected, all people, all animals, the planet, and the stars.

I became aware that there exists another dimension that lives within where everything is love and any form or thoughts of darkness and negativity do not exist. Once in that dimension of love, all that is true is love and nothing else. The light is love and does not know darkness. This was my answer to the question of how we reach a state of joy, fly above the clouds, crack the veil that separates the illusionary world we live in with the essence of all which love is.

I felt humbled after this revelation. The expansion of my understanding of reality in that moment was juxtaposed to how we live our daily lives that is full of judgment and ignorance. The need to catch myself when I start to judge others and remind myself of the love that heals all, became a priority. It is not easy to reach a continuous level of unconditional love but the opportunities through the challenges we face, help in our growth towards the light.

Once back in Las Vegas, I was asked to help collect donations of items to help in the construction of the actual sanctuary. I was given a long list which included a large amount of lumber and plywood that was going to be used to build the animal clinic plus the dogs' and cats' housing. Also, on the list was an X-Ray machine, and surgical tables among many other items. I was a bit concerned about how I was going to be able to fulfill such a request. I went to sleep that night determined that the following day was going to be the day to try. Regardless of the outcome, I was going to give it my all, pick up that phone and reach out.

Right before waking, in the in-between state before being fully awake, I had an odd dream that felt very real. I saw a small being, maybe three feet tall with large blue eyes and blond hair. His head was a little larger than normal. He seemed to be a child but behaved as an adult. His features were human but had an unearthly look about him. He had the sweetest smile and was beaming with light. His eyes sparkled while he looked at me.

I then became fully awake, but his magic and presence remained. I felt confident, at peace and eager to begin the project. The effect of the dream was so strong that I could not help but think that maybe my guides were there to support me.

As soon as I was ready, I grabbed the list of items to retrieve and began calling. This was in the 1980s so there was no internet or Google to help in the search. I did have a telephone directory that came in very handy. To my astonishment, every single person and corporation I called was ready to provide the items I was requesting. All I had to say was that I was calling on behalf of an animal rescue group that had acquired land in Arizona and was in the process of building a sanctuary for abandoned dogs and cats. I told the people I called that we needed certain items to start building the clinic and housing for the animals and medical equipment. I reached out to the biggest lumber manufacturer in Arizona who said that they would deliver all the lumber and plywood that we needed from their Phoenix location. I then called a clinic that donated an older X-Ray machine and a surgical table. Every single call I made, the person at the other end of the conversation was super helpful and kind. One item after the other on the list was donated. By late afternoon, it was done. As soon as the list was completed, the magic in the air stopped. It did feel as if I was being helped on another level. It was the smoothest, most uplifting experience I ever had asking for donations. I sometimes wonder who was that little being with the big blue eyes.

By 1991, Four Paws Animal Sanctuary was highly active rescuing animals as a No-kill animal sanctuary for unwanted pets. Until that time, I was busy fundraising for the sanctuary and starting a pet therapy program in Las Vegas for seniors in assisted living homes. Since my life-changing experience in Jerusalem, I knew that there was a presence guiding my spiritual life. I was always given signs and shown the way. My time in Las Vegas was productive and positive but I knew deep within that I had reached the last scene of the movie I was acting out. It was not easy making the decision since I had been with the community for thirteen years of my life and had gone through many challenges and growth.

One night, I decided to go out and sit under the stars in our backyard by our water fountain. Suddenly, unexpectedly, the energy changed. I knew that a strong presence had come to give me a message. It was a little frightening because the reality I was in at that moment had shifted and the darkness of the night was illuminated. I was being shown the last page of a screenplay where it was written in large capital letters "THE END."

I quickly went back inside but all I could see and hear was "This movie is over; the end." My knowingness within, or maybe my guides were showing me the similarity of life in this reality to acting out a role in a movie with a variety of characters. When we take a step back and watch the drama of life unfold, it looks very much like a movie with every character playing their role for an ultimate purpose. This was validated by my experience that night. It was clear that my time with "Four Paws" was now over.

At that time, my parents and sister were living in Los Angeles. I had an idea that maybe the best transition for me would be to move to Los Angeles and start a "Four Paws" outreach in the city. My idea was not received with open arms, but I was not prevented in my attempt to create a "Four Paws" outreach in Los Angeles.

Once I got to Los Angeles, I started going to street fairs and grocery stores and gave out brochures describing the work being done at Four Paws Animal Retreat in Arizona. I did not ask for donations, but I did begin a mailing list of the people who were interested in the work of Four Paws. During the next few months, I kept in touch with some community members and updated them on what I was doing.

One time, I came across a store and after I told the owner about the sanctuary, he suggested that I leave a jar and information about Four Paws to collect donations from their customers. I mentioned to one of the community members about the jar and he was quite thrilled. After a couple of weeks, I went by the store to see how they were doing with the jar and I was told that someone stole it with all the money in it. I immediately called my contact at the sanctuary and told him about it. Soon after, I got a phone call from someone at the sanctuary in Arizona requesting the mailing list I had put together and to inform me that they were going to take over for me from that moment on and continue the work that I had started. Someone stealing the jar was the last straw. I guess starting a Four Paws outreach in Los Angeles was not such a bad idea. I planted the seed and they made it come to fruition. Through their hard work, I am happy to report that they have since been quite effective in saving thousands of dogs' and cats' lives in the Los Angeles area.

I did return to Las Vegas a few months later to take my dog to my favorite homeopathic Vet. The community members in Las Vegas invited me to stay overnight in my old room. In the morning when I woke up, I get out of bed and put the blanket aside. I noticed that I had slept with a black widow spider under the cover next to my feet. It was a miracle that it did not bite me. I took it as a sign that my time with the organization was over.

Los Angeles

1991

ONCE IN LOS ANGELES, MY search for answers and understanding of the beyond and meaning of it all continued. I started visiting different spiritual communities and attending lectures about metaphysical subjects. After spending thirteen years as part of a spiritual community that believed that the teachings and truths given to them were the one and only and that they themselves were special as a result, that mindset became part of my reality.

To my surprise, when I started visiting other communities, and attending their lectures and classes, I found they all believed that they were the only ones who had all the answers, they were the ones with the truth about life and were special as a result. It was a bit of an eye-opener for me. I realized then that even spiritual communities had egos. They all thought that they were "the" elected ones with the only path to the one that was the source of all goodness and truth, the creator of all that is. I became aware that I had to listen and find the truth that resonated within myself. It is not about blindly following another because they are certain in what they believe. Be open to what the other has to say and then find the place inside of you that knows. I knew that anything that sought to instill fear was not coming from the light or the consciousness of love that I had experienced at different times in my life.

The same truth can be delivered by different sounding voices and appearances. It is received by us with the understanding that comes from our consciousness and energy vibration of our being. What was relevant to me was whether the message was coming from of place of love or fear. The light of the one only knows love. Fear is created from darkness and ignorance. We all have an internal voice, you can call it your higher self, God, the Light, or your internal GPS. It is always on, we must listen, connect with it and be aware. We all have a choice; do we surrender our power to others or listen within. Discover your true divine power and use it to bring change to the world.

It was 1995, and I found an ad in the paper for a free Introductory lecture to the teachings of Kabbalah. The location was close to where I lived in the San Fernando Valley of Los Angeles, and the topic spiked an interest in me. I knew practically nothing about Kabbalah. I had not thought about it since my friend had introduced me to it all those years ago in New York. All I knew was that it had Jewish roots. I always considered myself a cultural Jew but stayed far away from the religious part of it and its rules.

I arrived at the location and it was standing room only. A young man, maybe in his 20s or early 30s, began the lecture by explaining that Kabbalah is an ancient spiritual wisdom that can improve our lives and helps us to achieve fulfillment and find our purpose in life. He mentioned that in the past, Kabbalah was only available to scholarly married men over forty and that the founders of the Kabbalah Center were making the wisdom accessible and understandable to anyone, regardless of race, gender or religious belief. He continued, explaining many key points about what Kabbalah can teach us.

The explanations were simple and relevant to anyone asking

themselves the questions of what life is all about. At the end of the lecture, I left feeling that I wanted to learn more about the wisdom, but the classes were being held a bit far from where I lived, so I put the idea on a back burner.

Months later, I get a notice in the mail about a Kabbalistic astrologer giving readings at the Kabbalah Center in Los Angeles. I was interested, so I made the effort to drive a little farther to have an astrology reading. After the reading, I find out that they recently opened a Center in the Encino neighborhood of the San Fernando Valley, near where I lived in Sherman Oaks. It did not take me long to decide to sign up for a Kabbalah 1 course.

I started taking Kabbalah 1 and found it to clarify the rules of the universe and on how to bring more positivity into my life. I continued with Kabbalah 2 and began applying the rules of life that I was learning to my daily life with many positive results.

Every Saturday morning, the Los Angeles Center had services which included a reading from the Torah and lunch afterwards. I always stayed away from anything that seemed religious, but I decided to be open and go. Once there, I found everyone to be friendly and helpful. The appearance of the service seemed like a regular religious service but the explanations I received for why everything was done were quite different. Most religious places of worship go through their rituals in a robotic way. What I was learning at the Kabbalah Center was that the purpose of it all was to help people get closer and connect to the light which was the energy of unconditional love.

After the service, I stayed for lunch which was held in the auditorium and ran into Herb, my Kabbalah teacher from the Valley. He asked me if I wanted to meet Rav Berg and his wife Karen, the founders of the Center who had made Kabbalah available to everyone. The Rav, as he was called, was sitting with Karen at one of the tables in the auditorium.

Herb walked me to the Rav and told him that I was a new Kabbalah student. Rav Berg turned and looked at me. He did not say a word. Just gave me a gentle acknowledgement. I was ready to tell him it was an honor to meet him, but I could not get the words out. At that moment, my whole being was filled with a sensation of joy. My face had the biggest smile which was generated by the immense feeling of happiness that I felt. I wanted to talk but I literally could not. I wanted to stop smiling but the feeling of joy overpowered me. I kept on thinking, who was this man that just by being in his presence, had lifted me to a place of joy. The whole meeting lasted maybe three minutes, but the experience has remained with me ever since.

It was 1996, and I continued taking Kabbalah classes in the Valley. That year, I decided to travel to New York to attend the Kabbalah Centre's International Rosh Hashana Event. Rosh Hashana is the Jewish New Year which usually falls sometime in September. According to Kabbalah, during that time, there are cosmic openings that provide all of humanity, not only the Jews, opportunities to draw certain blessings into our lives. During Rosh Hashana, we can awaken the light that can remove all judgment created by our negative actions.

I arrived at the hotel the day before the event. I walked in and the lobby was busy with people from all over the world who had just arrived to participate in the New Year celebration. I was a bit jet lagged from my trip so I decided to go to sleep early so I could be ready for the event the following day.

It was right before dawn when I saw the Rav right outside my hotel window. He was shining bright with a most beautiful smile. *How could that be if my hotel room was on an upper floor?* He seemed to be floating in the air with arms extended welcoming me to the Center and the special event. He then floated right through the window towards me.

I woke up and his image faded away, but his presence remained as a strong memory in my soul.

I've been a Kabbalah student for more than twenty years. The teachings of Kabbalah have undeniably helped me to understand the meaning and purpose of life and showed me the importance of treating others with human dignity and respect. I still follow my internal GPS and listen to the voice within which guides me with love and peace. I continue to, at times, explore other teachings and find how so many spiritual paths are connected.

One time during a guided meditation at the Center, I was asked to connect to a place that was significant in my life. In my meditation, I traveled to Jerusalem where I first encountered the powerful being that changed the direction of my life. I then traveled to Tsfat, a mystical place in Israel where the Rav is buried. I wanted to visit the Rav. As I entered the cave where he is buried, the cave lit up and all I heard was the Rav laughing with so much joy that I was quickly engulfed in a state of pure joy. His laughter was so powerful that I instantly knew that he was telling me that his being exists in joy and that his message for me was the importance to connect to the joy and love that is the essence of what lies beyond the veil of our existence. It is not an easy concept to grasp that the physical reality we live in is an illusion. It is there for us to play the game of life in order to allow us to reach our next level of development which brings us closer to our essence which is one of love.

Conclusion

How do we bring our spiritual experiences that lead to an awakening of love into our everyday lives? Once back in Los Angeles, after years of living outside the box, I found myself returning to a reality I once faced, but this time with a knowledge and an awareness of purpose that I previously lacked.

In our daily lives, we are constantly asked to make a choice, do we make choices based on our inclination of fear and selfishness or is there another path that will ultimately bring peace and well being for the greater good of all including myself. One of my greatest realizations is that self-absorption leads to pain and suffering and creates veils around our inner light. When we put our attention outside of ourselves, with the intention of sharing and helping others, we tear the veils and become connected to the essence of the Light which is one of peace and love.

While I was writing this, I glanced out my window and saw my neighbor's dog running in the street by himself with his leash on. I dropped what I was doing and ran outside because I sensed that something was off. I go outside and suddenly the dog runs towards me and I was able to grab his leash. Shortly after, my neighbor appears, out of breath, obviously chasing after the dog. When he saw that I was holding on to his dog and he was safe, a beautiful smile came over him. He expressed his gratitude and we both left happy. This is only a small example of the effect of choosing not to think only of oneself and putting our attention out to share with others. A seed of kindness goes a long way. Your act of kindness, along with a feeling of gratitude and appreciation, might be the seed that will tip the scales and bring more positive energy to our world.

I have a tendency of finding joy when I go beyond my Ego self and bring an awareness and understanding to others that transforms their pain into one of peace and happiness. Once back in Los Angeles, after my path of exploration of the beyond, I was led into the teaching profession. I was given the great responsibility to educate children not only to academic subjects but also the importance of treating each other with dignity and respect. Watching how conflicts can arise between our youth, inspired me to create Teach the Children Peace Foundation, a nonprofit that supports programs that give children the skills and tools they need to bring resolution to conflict through nonviolent methods.

We all have our individual path to fulfillment. The path I have chosen has given me glimpses of what I consider the true reality we are all attempting to reach. Eventually, we will all reach our ultimate destination, and return to our true home, a place where fear and hatred do not exist. A place that only knows love.

And the journey continues…

Photo Collage

1977 New York, NY

Publicist for the Broadway show "Golda" with Golda Meir, Prime Minister of Israel at an opening night celebration for the staff of the show.

Picture of Golda's cup, fork and cigarette butts after she left.

Silvia Perchuk, 1977 New York, NY

Publicist for the Miss Universe Pageant after Miss USA left a Photo shoot, the photographer wanted to take pictures of me with the Miss USA crown and sash as a memory of my work promoting the event.

The name of the photographer who took picture of Silvia with the Miss USA crown and sash.

PHOTOGRAPH © BY HELEN MARCUS
120 EAST 75th STREET
NEW YORK, N.Y. 10021
TR 9-6903
NOT TO BE REPRODUCED OR USED IN ANY FORM
WITHOUT PHOTOGRAPHER'S WRITTEN CONSENT.

1979 Dallas, Texas
Clown Ministry

Red Rock Canyon

Poppy the Clown

Silvia and Henry

Teach the Children Peace
Vision Board Workshop